FROM HOMEMAKER TO HOMEPRENEUR

7 Secrets to Earn Money & Improve the Quality of Your Life

FROM HOMEMAKER TO HOMEPRENEUR

7 Secrets to Earn Money & Improve the Quality of Your Life

By

PRITESH SHAH

Worldwide Published by

Pendown Press

PENDOWN PRESS

An ISO 9001 & ISO 14001 Certified Co.,
Regd. Office: 2525/193, 1st Floor, Onkar Nagar-A,
Tri Nagar, Delhi-110035
Ph.: 09350849407, 09312235086
E-mail: info@pendownpress.com
Branch Office: 1A/2A, 20, Hari Sadan, Ansari Road,
Daryaganj, New Delhi-110002
Ph.: 011-45794768
Website: PendownPress.com

First Edition: 2020

ISBN: 978-93-90479-04-7

Layout and Cover Designed by Pendown Graphics Team
Printed and Bound in India by Thomson Press India Ltd.

CONTENTS

INTRODUCTION

Before I start with my introduction, I wish to tell you a short story.

It was 6 AM, Anjali woke up and went for a shower. She started making breakfast for her family; meanwhile, she collected the newspaper and milk. She dropped off the kids for the school bus and started preparing tea for her in-laws and lunch for her husband. She began cleaning the house, and by noon, she completed the laundry. In the evening she went for grocery shopping and then started preparing dinner as she reached home. Finishing the dinner, she cleaned the kitchen and did the dishes once again. And finally, a Goodnight.

Are you too like Anjali? Is your routine like the one I just explained? If your answer to these questions is an emphatic yes, then you're reading the right book. Today, this book will clear all of your doubts. Your routine is going to change. You will witness more comfort, diverse knowledge and excellent command over yourself.

Hello, I am Pritesh Shah, a passionate businessman, dream- fulfilling expert and a personality performance coach.

My qualifications say that I am a Civil Engineer, but I feel I am more than that, much more. I followed my engineering by joining a construction business which went on for nine years. There was a constant belief in me that said something was missing. So, for following that belief, I started taking Transformation Courses. As I completed them, I got to know: what I love the most is learning and teaching new things to make a DIFFERENCE.

It has been 20 years I have been following my passion for making a difference via Direct Selling and Performance coaching. I have learnt beautiful things from experts like Shiv Khera, Darren Hardy and many more.

You have to believe me when I say that in these 20 years I have seen people go from 10 to a 100! And to remark it, most of these were housewives/homemakers at one time, just like you are right now. My wife, Purvi Shah, is yet another example of a housewife turned into an entrepreneur. She is my partner in the business we do; she is my better half and deserves all the credits.

I duly respect the compassion and love you have for your family, but I can also see your unfulfilled dreams.

Even though this easy guide is for the Homemakers, the students can also learn from this and gain value for starting their business or initiative. Students are burdened with academics. Thus, for the growing world, they should learn work-study and work-life balance at an early age. This book will help them prioritize their goals and clear the myths they have.

Let me tell you- you're not alone in this. There are lakhs of people like you, waiting for a solution!

So, here is this book! This book will solve all your problems; it will encourage you, ask you your goals and passion to achieve those goals!

But, before you know and prioritize your goals, you might not be able to feel what this book says. So, I request you to "Tick" the Options that you like and want to have, below:

(Remember, there is NO LIMIT, you can tick as many as you wish!)

- Earning 10,000 to 10,00,000 Rs. per month
- Health and Fitness
- Recognition
- Best Education Plan for Children
- Foreign Trips
- New House
- Renovation of house
- Cars
- Jewellery
- Fancy Shopping
- Laptops
- Luxurious Smartphone
- Improved relationships

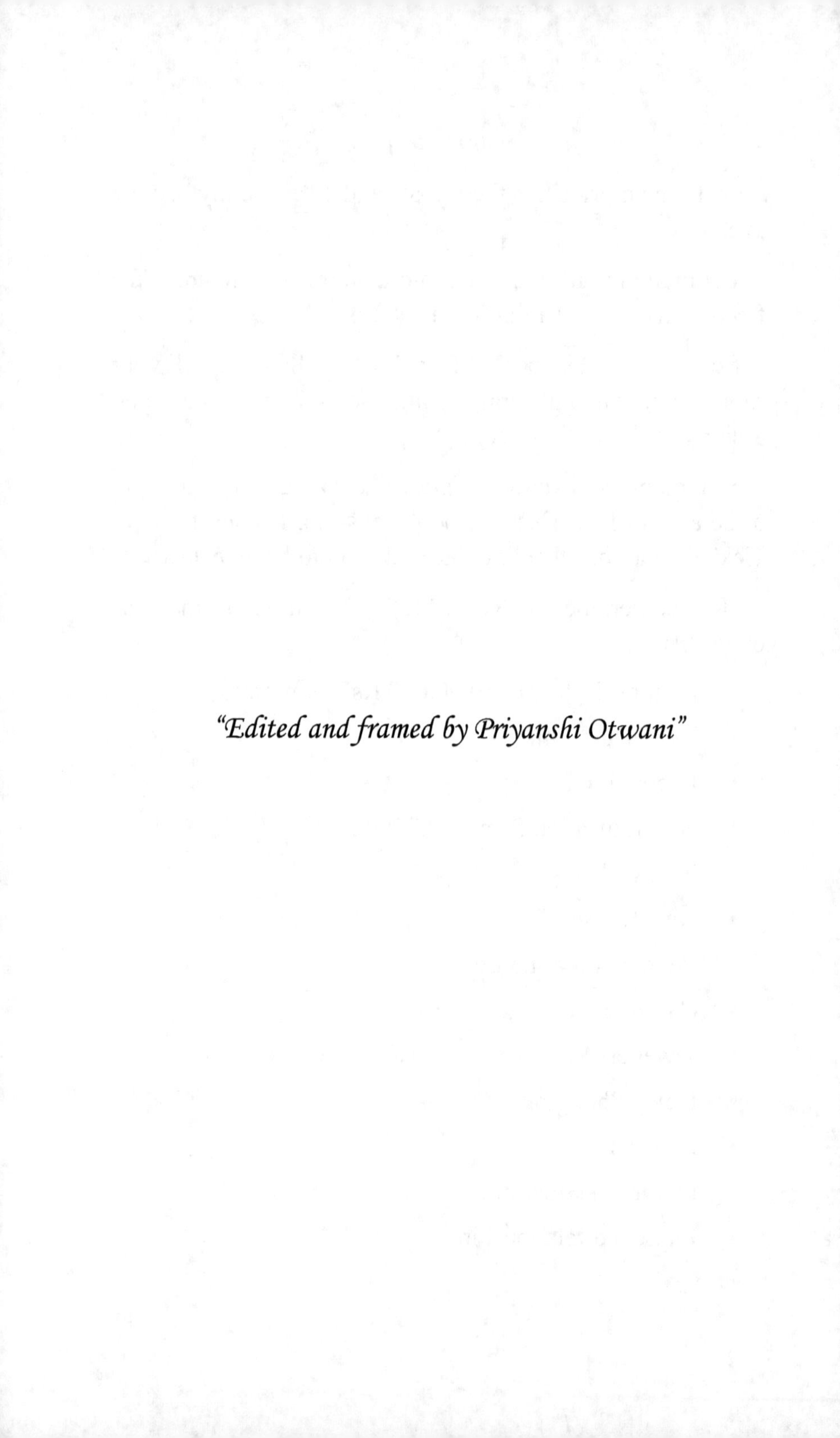

"Edited and framed by Priyanshi Otwani"

Chapter 1

WHAT ARE THE COMMON BELIEFS THAT STOP WOMEN FROM LIVING A LIFE THEY WANT?

What are the common points that keep women away from achieving what they want? Why do they always hesitate to take new adventures? It is because, these common beliefs are just one-sided. These beliefs are the creation of their over-thinking. Our homemakers are comfortable in creating such beliefs for themselves, which eventually stop them from living a sparkling life.

I am not important!

Let me present to you a simple analogy, so that you can

understand your actual worth in this world of your dreams.

- There are two types of earrings— one is metal made, and other has solitaire/diamonds. We all know which one is more important and precious. Now, most of the housewives consider themselves to be metal earrings. However, they should count themselves as Diamonds or Solitaire earrings. Highly important and precious.

- I have seen women always putting their families first. This behaviour could be out of love for them, but mostly it is because they don't consider themselves important enough.

- In this process, she forgets that she too needs fuel to run. And this fuel is her improved lifestyle.

- And, today I want a promise from you ALL, that you would consider yourself as the SOLITAIRE Earrings instead of metal earrings. In fact, you are much more precious than a Solitaire.

I am not capable

- In India, many families are male-dominated. Male domination has somehow made women feel incapable of certain things in life.

- And sometimes this becomes the end of your self-esteem forever.

- But I am not going to let you dim your inner light. You are capable of everything, and you should know that very well.

- Do you remember that one fine time you almost gave up? You thought you wouldn't be able to cross something, but with sheer will and focus you DID IT! Just like you have demonstrated this dedication in past, you can do it now as well!

You become what you think. So, you have to start believing that you are capable. And eventually you will become capable.

Lack of support

When I talk about lack of support, I don't mean that there is no one to support housewives. I mean, there is support but the women aren't acknowledging it.

- They might be getting support of 6 out 10 people, but inside their heart they still feel unsupported.

- You believe that emotional and moral support is always a lacking element. But this is only on your side. Again, if you stop thinking this way, and turn to positive roads, and ask for help, you will be surely starting something new.

- Sheetal too believed that she wasn't supported enough. But the moment she took it in positive way and reached out for help/advice, she became her own boss! She is now working like a professional entrepreneur, isn't that amazing?

- There is abundance of support if you are willing to search for it! Just reach out to people and they will be ready to support you!

Chapter 2

WHAT ARE THE FEARS STOPPING YOU FROM TAKING ACTION FOR INDEPENDENCE?

It is completely natural to have fears. It is in human nature. But, what is not fine, is not taking any action to overcome that fear. The real courage would be to take a step, even when you have fears. That's the only way to overcome your fears. You have overcome many such fears in past as well, like your wedding, or starting a new life with In-laws, all these steps made you nervous at first, but you made through these, right? So, you can do this now as well!

I haven't done this work before, how will I learn?

- If you're worried about the working process, there are plenty of educational courses available online.

- The Covid-19 has already changed our working and learning environment. Everything is online now.

- So, what's better than online learning and online business in such times? You can freely avail any online course that provides you skills and value addition.

- You can learn from home, without dedicating any fixed hours or strict regime.

- Many supportive teachers will teach you the skills that would help you understand various aspects of business or the networking or earning.

- In online learning, you get to meet many enthusiastic students, just like you, from around the world!

I need to sell the products

- Under-confidence is a highly common fear that people face.

- In many online business opportunities, you don't even have to sell products. In modern business era, you create a buying environment.

- We should not sell, people would buy.

- And how is that possible? Well, you have to understand the products and recommend them with your honest reviews. This will give you an opportunity to become professional consultant.

- In life, when you want to achieve something extra, you have to work a little extra.

FACT - You don't even have to sell all the products, only the ones that you have used and you can recommend.

What if I am not comfortable in talking to people?

- I completely understand that many housewives and students have an introvert personality. They don't speak in groups much.

- If that is so, then this industry is just right for you! You can do your business sitting at home using a smartphone or laptop, and you don't need to talk to anyone or join any gatherings.

- Sounds perfect for your introvert personality, right?

I have small kids and many responsibilities, so I would not be able to do any business

Having to manage small kids and an entire family becomes a tedious job in itself. And you have been successful in managing that job so far.

- So, if I am not wrong, you already have managerial skills. All you need to do is, to use such skills in your business and you are good to go!

- And what if you could become a "mompreneur"? Yes, you read that correct! Many businesses are offering flexible working hours, along with working from home!

I don't have educational qualifications, how can I do business?

Many people consider educational qualifications to be of very high importance. And in some cases it might be right as well.

But in Online Business, there are absolutely no rules and restrictions for these.

- I would say, if you have this concern, then direct selling is the best option for you. In direct selling businesses, you will have various offers of learning an in-depth syllabus. Just like in school/college, there is a syllabus, you will have a set of learnings here as well.

- The students of undergraduate programs and the housewives who are not having higher degrees need not worry about this aspect at all.

- You are welcomed with any educational qualifications; the coaches only need your passion!

I already have a good degree, then why should I do this business?

This pandemic has already taught us what losing job, business, and savings can do to us.

- If you're a housewife with a higher educational degree, then you must start a business soon. Why? Because you're already aware of many business aspects, you have communication skills. So it will be a little easier for you to have a grasp over activities.

- And if you are good at it, then a big business might offer you huge deals!

I do not know how to work online

Most of you use Facebook and Instagram very easily. Who taught you how to use these? No , right? You just started using because of your interest.

- But here, you'll be having very friendly teachers who will teach you every single step.

- Students, housewives, or anyone who wishes to learn and earn without compromising their family time, can join online training programs.

- The comprehensive programs will teach everything about online business and online selling as well. Also, many courses offer you skill-based business.

- These would teach you personality grooming, communication skills, etc. and then you would be ready to take off on your business plane!

Chapter 3

MYTHS ABOUT THE NETWORK MARKETING INDUSTRY

With network marketing flourishing day by day, the doubts and myth regarding the same are increasing too. Let me discuss major myths with you.

There are fixed targets in network marketing

- I cannot stress on this enough that network marketing doesn't have fixed targets. It doesn't pressurize you to work 10 hours a day and sell so and so number of products. Not at all.

- I have been doing network marketing for 20 years now, and I did not face a single day when someone gave me a target.

- You can do business on your convenient timings and willingness.

It is difficult to earn in the network marketing business!

- Well, if you agree to the line above, allow me to explain why it is a false belief.

- First of all, network marketing requires minimum investment, compared to the capital investment required in other start-ups or new businesses.

- Secondly, in direct selling companies or system-based companies, it is easy to earn (because there are no middle-men). So, you can stay assured of the ROI (Return on Investment).

- Now, if you allow me, I would like to inform you that in these years, I have seen housewives earning 30,000 to 50,000 Rs in 5-6 months of business, and eventually earning 4 to 5 lakhs a month in 4-5 years. So, what is stopping you?

Products are expensive in a network marketing business

- Many people belonging from middle-class families, be it students or housewives, believe that products in network marketing are usually expensive. However, in reality, it is not correct.

- The well-known companies running on network marketing or direct selling, follow the rules under section 105 A by Indian Government, so the products cannot be expensive.

- Further, the commodities of these brands, are "value for money products."In simple words, these products offer you quality and lasting results.

  So, even if you are a student with limited pocket money, you can delay your Starbucks coffee for a week, and put that sum in your healthy business!

Chapter 4

WHAT ARE THE CHALLENGES YOU FACE? HOW TO OVERCOME THEM?

Human beings have been facing challenges since the time immemorial. We have an innate ability to overcome the challenges either by hardwork or smartwork. With sheer dedication and perseverance, you can break down the walls of challenges!

I am new in the city; I don't know many people here.

- People often keep changing cities due to their partner's shifting or any other reason. But that should not stop you from starting something good for yourself.

- Rinku, a smart lady from Mumbai, married Gunjan from Ahmedabad. She shifted to Ahmedabad, and her concern was the same. "I don't know anyone in this city". It has been ten years she is working, and now she knows more number of people in this city than Gunjan does.

- You see, the power of network marketing? A young lady, in a new city, creates a network of people that even we don't know. That was possible because Rinku took her decision. She followed her dreams, and so can you!

What if my family members don't allow me for the business?

- When I said you should be capable of deciding for yourself, I did not mean you should go and fight with your family to start a business. No, that's not right.

- You should calmly and patiently explain them the opportunities, chances, and the future benefits of the venture.

- And I believe that if you have deep dedication, you will be able to explain your family and you will eventually start the business!

I don't have money to start the business/I don't want to invest early

- To be honest, in some businesses, you might need to invest, but, many business enterprises don't require any prior investments from your side.

- First, you need to undergo educational training, and

then you can start earning. Isn't it a good idea? To learn new things and gain without investing. Many students face this problem of investment.

- Online business or education-based business is a feasible solution for them too!

Chapter 5

LESSONS YOU SHOULD LEARN FROM MY MISTAKES

I am not perfect. I have made some mistakes in my career that I could have avoided. But, the silver lining is- I got a lot to learn from my mistakes, and today I have got a chance to share those mistakes with you so that you too can take a lesson before starting your business.

Not considering Direct Selling to be a massive industry or a great opportunity.

- In the initial months of our business, I did not consider direct selling to be a huge opportunity. I did not pay much attention to long-term investments, or the products that I was using. That was my first mistake.

- Later on, realizing this, I started using more products that would eventually be recommended by me. I worked on paid advertisements, digital platforms, and I saw steep growth.

- Direct selling, in today's date, is one of the best opportunities present in the market. And if you consider the facts published, the worth of direct selling industry in India has crossed a whopping mark of 13,000 Crore Rs. And, in direct selling, the "wellness" category is the largest segment, contributing 33% share of sales.

Not paying attention to pieces of the training

- When I started the business, my focus was on networking and marketing. I wanted to become successful. As a result, I couldn't pay much attention to the training.

- And, training is the most vital part of any skill/ education-based earnings. If you are not thorough with the subjects, you cannot teach others the same.

  Thus, before you focus on earning or marketing, make sure you learn your courses carefully.

Lack of knowledge about products

- Diving into a massive business, I was very excited to work with different people. Considering the opportunity I had got, I took working very seriously, because of which I skipped learning about the products in-depth.

- You need to use the products to understand their attributes and benefits. Then and then only you can recommend a product to your network.

- So, you must invest time in the "self-usage" of products, to achieve better results.

Delayed learning the digital marketing platforms

- Twenty years ago, social media marketing or digital marketing wasn't the term around. I was working solely on an offline basis which continued for a long time. Later on, I observed the power of digital media.

- Digital marketing can take your business from 0 to 100! All you need to do is to learn digital marketing. Once you have learnt, you can start your experiments and trials.

- Right now, there are 1000+ trainees, and students learning from my digital portal every month!

- All you need for online business and learning, is a smartphone and internet connection, that's it! You are good to go!

  So you noticed the power of digital marketing tools!

Chapter 6

WHO IS THE PERSON STOPPING YOU?

- There is a significant element stopping you from achieving your dreams, your goals. And that element is a person. Yes, a person who always doubts your potential and dedication. Can you guess who this person might be? No? I'll tell you. It is YOU. Yes, you are the only person between you and your goals.

- You are the only one who can either make it or break it. The decision is always in your hand. You do HAVE A CHOICE.

- So, never complain that you do not have any options. Because, if there is a will, there's a way! And I can assure you of that.

- "I cannot do this, I don't know how to do this, people would not support me, I will probably fail..." etc. is all in your head. These are all just the results of fear and overthinking. You have to open doors to positive thoughts. If so many people can win it, why can't you?

You may name a person's success as miracle, luck or destiny. But in reality, success is achieved only when you earn it yourself! No one serves you a platter of achievements in this world. Hardworking, smart working and ethical approach can take you to the highest peak of your career.

Chapter 7

WHEN TO START?

- After discussing the various opportunities for housewives and homemakers, the important question that arises is–when should I start? Well, starting is the only courageous step you'll have to make in your career. It is all about the first step. Once you take your first step, then nothing can stop you. When you think of past, you may think of the ditched chances and regret that. So, you should not repeat that mistake now, else you'll regret this as well.

- When a chance knocks at your door, you answer it. Let's know why? Because in online education-based earning, you have no risk at all. You are playing a game at no loss. So, even if things don't work in future, or you don't like it, you can stop it whenever you wish.

Isn't that advantageous? How many businesses offer you this Freedom?

- Start with anything that stirs passion in you. That fuels your energy and creativity. Please don't sit back and be baffled with questions, it is never too late. Kill your hesitation and say hello to bright future. Right time is when you take a step towards your dreams!

If I talk about myself, I have been very fortunate that I accepted this opportunity on right time. If I had not done so, I wouldn't have been here, writing this book and encouraging thousands of potential homepreneurs!

The right time to start is NOW!

CONCLUSION

Friends, if you have read this book till here, please do a little more and read till the very end.

Till now, we have covered:

What are the common beliefs that stop women from living a life they want?

What are the fears stopping you from taking action?

Myths about the Network Marketing Industry

What are the challenges you face? How to overcome them?

Lessons you should learn from my mistakes

Who is the person stopping you?

When to start?

I have a remarkable feeling that after reading this book, you will too start something new, something important, and something that gives you a sense of ENTERPRENEURSHIP!

Today, with this book, I want to help you become a better version of yourself. I want you to take every sentence of this book, seriously. Please do not take any decision on hassle. I want you to think about it and to discuss this with your family and friends.

If at any point in life, you need help, you can look around; you can find many people like me. And **if you need my help** with your better and independent future, **I am always here**. I am just a call away!

You can search for many such online opportunities, and you will definitely find many as well. You should **start something that makes you happy and keeps you active**. However, if you still feel a need to know more about our opportunity, you can freely contact us via below- mentioned details. We will send you a **FREE link of** Webinar which is scheduled at 5PM every day.

Available options to reach us are given below:

https://www.facebook.com/purvipritesh/

Instagram.com/pritesh_shah2000

http://linkedin.com/in/

Wait, wait….wait!

Where are you going? Don't keep this book down just yet.

I wanted to share a very important Quote with you all. Because, it was written for everyone like you:

मंजिल उन्हीं को मिलती है, जिनके सपनों में जान होती है,
पंख से कुछ नहीं होता, हौसलों से उड़ान होती है!!

I wish you all the best for your future. May you achieve your goals!